Cram101 Textbook Outlines to accompany:

Intellectual Property: The Law of Trademarks, Copyrights, Patents, and Trad

Deborah E. Bouchoux, 3rd Edition

A Cram101 Inc. publication (c) 2011.

Cram101 Textbook Outlines and Cram101.com are Cram101 Inc. publications and services. All notes, highlights, reviews, and practice tests are written and prepared by Cram101, all rights reserved.

PRACTICE EXAMS.

Get all of the self-teaching practice exams for each chapter of this textbook at **www.Cram101.com** and ace the tests. Here is an example:

Chapter 1

Intellectual Property: The Law of Trademarks, Copyrights, Patents, and Trad
Deborah E. Bouchoux, 3rd Edition,
All Material Written and Prepared by Cram101

I WANT A BETTER GRADE. Items 1 - 50 of 100.

1. _____ gives the creator of an original work exclusive right for a certain time period in relation to that work, including its publication, distribution and adaptation; after which time the work is said to enter the public domain. _____ applies to any expressible form of an idea or information that is substantive and discrete and fixed in a medium. Some jurisdictions also recognize "moral rights" of the creator of a work, such as the right to be credited for the work.

   ○ Copyright ○ C corporation
   ○ Cable theft ○ Cadbury Report

2. The United States _____, a part of the Library of Congress, is the official U.S. government body that maintains records of copyright registration in the United States. It is used by copyright title searchers who are attempting to clear a chain of title for copyrighted works.

   The head of the _____ is called the Register of Copyrights.

   ○ Copyright Office ○ C corporation
   ○ Cable theft ○ Cadbury Report

3. _____ are legal property rights over creations of the mind, both artistic and commercial, and the corresponding fields of law. Under _____ law, owners are granted certain exclusive rights to a variety of intangible assets, such as musical, literary, and artistic works; ideas, discoveries and inventions; and words, phrases, symbols, and designs. Common types of _____ include copyrights, trademarks, patents, industrial design rights and trade secrets.

You get a 50% discount for the online exams. Go to **Cram101.com**, click Sign Up at the top of the screen, and enter DK73DW5677 in the promo code box on the registration screen. Access to Cram101.com is $4.95 per month, cancel at any time.

With Cram101.com online, you also have access to extensive reference material.

You will nail those essays and papers. Here is an example from a Cram101 Biology text:

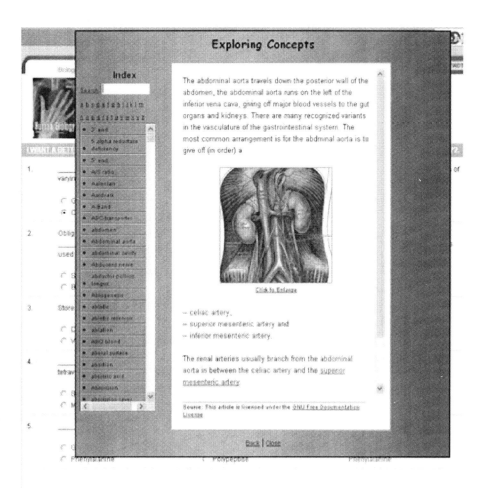

Visit **www.Cram101.com**, click Sign Up at the top of the screen, and enter DK73DW5677 in the promo code box on the registration screen. Access to www.Cram101.com is normally $9.95 per month, but because you have purchased this book, your access fee is only $4.95 per month, cancel at any time. Sign up and stop highlighting textbooks forever.

Learning System

Cram101 Textbook Outlines is a learning system. The notes in this book are the highlights of your textbook, you will never have to highlight a book again.

How to use this book. Take this book to class, it is your notebook for the lecture. The notes and highlights on the left hand side of the pages follow the outline and order of the textbook. All you have to do is follow along while your instructor presents the lecture. Circle the items emphasized in class and add other important information on the right side. With Cram101 Textbook Outlines you'll spend less time writing and more time listening. Learning becomes more efficient.

Cram101.com Online

Increase your studying efficiency by using Cram101.com's practice tests and online reference material. It is the perfect complement to Cram101 Textbook Outlines. Use self-teaching matching tests or simulate in-class testing with comprehensive multiple choice tests, or simply use Cram's true and false tests for quick review. Cram101.com even allows you to enter your in-class notes for an integrated studying format combining the textbook notes with your class notes.

Visit **www.Cram101.com**, click Sign Up at the top of the screen, and enter **DK73DW5677** in the promo code box on the registration screen. Access to www.Cram101.com is normally $9.95 per month, but because you have purchased this book, your access fee is only $4.95 per month. Sign up and stop highlighting textbooks forever.

Copyright © 2011 by Cram101, Inc. All rights reserved. "Cram101"® and "Never Highlight a Book Again!"® are registered trademarks of Cram101, Inc. ISBN(s): 9781616987633. EDx-6.2010111

Intellectual Property: The Law of Trademarks, Copyrights, Patents, and Trad
Deborah E. Bouchoux, 3rd

CONTENTS

1. Part I Introduction to Intellectual Property 2
2. Part II The Law of Trademarks 12
3. Part III The Law of Copyrights 38
4. Part IV The Law of Patents 62

Chapter 1. Part I Introduction to Intellectual Property

Copyright	Copyright gives the creator of an original work exclusive right for a certain time period in relation to that work, including its publication, distribution and adaptation; after which time the work is said to enter the public domain. Copyright applies to any expressible form of an idea or information that is substantive and discrete and fixed in a medium. Some jurisdictions also recognize "moral rights" of the creator of a work, such as the right to be credited for the work.
Copyright Office	The United States Copyright Office, a part of the Library of Congress, is the official U.S. government body that maintains records of copyright registration in the United States. It is used by copyright title searchers who are attempting to clear a chain of title for copyrighted works. The head of the Copyright Office is called the Register of Copyrights.
Intellectual property	Intellectual property are legal property rights over creations of the mind, both artistic and commercial, and the corresponding fields of law. Under intellectual property law, owners are granted certain exclusive rights to a variety of intangible assets, such as musical, literary, and artistic works; ideas, discoveries and inventions; and words, phrases, symbols, and designs. Common types of intellectual property include copyrights, trademarks, patents, industrial design rights and trade secrets.
Patent	A patent is a set of exclusive rights granted by a state to an inventor or his assignee for a limited period of time in exchange for a disclosure of an invention. The procedure for granting patent s, the requirements placed on the patent ee and the extent of the exclusive rights vary widely between countries according to national laws and international agreements. Typically, however, a patent application must include one or more claims defining the invention which must be new, inventive, and useful or industrially applicable.
Personal property	Personal property is a type of property. In the common law systems Personal property may also be called chattels or personalty. It is distinguished from real property, or real estate. Personal property may be classified in a variety of ways. Tangible Personal property refers to any type of property that can generally be moved (i.e., it is not attached to real property or land), touched or felt. These generally include items such as furniture, clothing, jewelry, art, writings, or household goods. In some cases, there can be formal title documents that show the ownership and transfer rights of that property after a person"s death (for example, motor vehicles, boats, etc.) In many cases, however, tangible Personal property will not be "titled" in an owner"s name and is presumed to be whatever property he or she was in possession of at the time of his or her death. Intangible Personal property or "intangibles" refers to Personal property that cannot actually be moved, touched or felt, but instead represents something of value such as negotiable instruments, securities, goods, and intangible assets including chose in action.
Real property	In the common law, real property refers to one of the three main classes of property, the other two classes being personal property and intellectual property. real property generally encompasses land, land improvements resulting from human effort including buildings and machinery sited on land, and various property rights over the preceding.

Chapter 1. Part I Introduction to Intellectual Property

Chapter 1. Part I Introduction to Intellectual Property

	The concept is variously named and defined in other jurisdictions: heritable property in Scotland, immobilier in France, and immovable property in Canada, United States, India, Pakistan, Bangladesh, Malta, Cyprus, and in countries where civil law systems prevail, including most of Europe, Russia, and South America.
Trade secret	A trade secret is a formula, practice, process, design, instrument, pattern by which a business can obtain an economic advantage over competitors or customers. In some jurisdictions, such secrets are referred to as "confidential information" or "classified information". The precise language by which a trade secret is defined varies by jurisdiction (as do the particular types of information that are subject to trade secret protection.)
Trademark	A trademark or trade mark is a distinctive sign or indicator used by an individual, business organization and to distinguish its products or services from those of other entities. A trademark is designated by the following symbols: • â„¢ (for an unregistered trademark that is, a mark used to promote or brand goods); • â„ (for an unregistered service mark, that is, a mark used to promote or brand services); and • Â® (for a registered trademark) A trademark is a type of intellectual property, and typically a name, word, phrase, logo, symbol, design, image, or a combination of these elements. There is also a range of non-conventional trademark s comprising marks which do not fall into these standard categories. The owner of a registered trademark may commence legal proceedings for trademark infringement to prevent unauthorized use of that trademark
Unfair competition	Unfair competition in commercial law can refer to any of various distinct areas of law which may give rise to distinct criminal offences and civil causes of action: • Matters pertaining to antitrust law, known in the European Union as competition law. • Unfair business practices such as fraud, misrepresentation, tortious interference, and unconscionable contracts and business practices. In the European Union, each member state must regulate unfair business practices in accordance with the principles laid down in the Unfair Commercial Practices Directive, subject to transitional periods. (.
Service mark	In some countries, notably the United States, a trademark used to identify a service rather than a product is called a Service mark or servicemark. When a Service mark is federally registered, the standard registration symbol Â® or "Reg U.S. Pat ' TM Off" may be used (the same symbol is used to mark registered trademarks.) Before it is registered, it is common practice (but has no legal standing) to use the Service mark symbol $^{\text{Service mark}}$ (a superscript Service mark.)

Chapter 1. Part I Introduction to Intellectual Property

Chapter 1. Part I Introduction to Intellectual Property

The Commerce Clause	The Commerce Clause is an enumerated power listed in the United States Constitution (Article 1, Section 8, Clause 3.) The clause states that Congress has the power to regulate commerce with foreign nations, among the states, and with the Native American tribes. Courts and commentators have tended to discuss each of these three areas of commerce as a separate power granted to the Congress of the United States.
Design patent	In the United States, a Design patent is a patent granted on the ornamental design of a functional item. Design patent s are a type of industrial design right. Ornamental designs of jewelry, furniture, beverage containers (see Fig.
Public domain	The Public domain is a range of abstract materials--commonly referred to as intellectual property-- which are not owned or controlled by anyone. The term indicates that these materials are therefore "public property", and available for anyone to use for any purpose. The Public domain can be defined in contrast to several forms of intellectual property; the Public domain in contrast to copyrighted works is different from the Public domain in contrast to trademarks or patented works.
United States Patent and Trademark Office	The United States Patent and Trademark Office is an agency in the United States Department of Commerce that issues patents to inventors and businesses for their inventions, and trademark registration for product and intellectual property identification. The USPTO is currently based in Alexandria, Virginia, after a 2006 move from the Crystal City area of Arlington, Virginia. The offices under Patents and the Chief Information Officer that remained just outside the southern end of Crystal City completed moving to Randolph Square, a brand new building in Shirlington Village, on 27 April 2009.
Utility	In economics, utility is a measure of the relative satisfaction from consumption of various goods and services. Given this measure, one may speak meaningfully of increasing or decreasing utility, and thereby explain economic behavior in terms of attempts to increase one"s utility. For illustrative purposes, changes in utility are sometimes expressed in units called utils.
Corporation	The institution most often referenced by the word "corporation" is a public or publicly traded corporation, the shares of which are traded on a public stock exchange (e.g., the New York Stock Exchange or Nasdaq in the United States) where shares of stock of corporations are bought and sold by and to the general public. Most of the largest businesses in the world are publicly traded corporations. However, the majority of corporations are said to be closely held, privately held or close corporations, meaning that no ready market exists for the trading of shares.
Department of Commerce	The United States Department of Commerce is the Cabinet department of the United States government concerned with promoting economic growth. It was originally created as the United States Department of Commerce and Labor on February 14, 1903. It was subsequently renamed to the Department of Commerce on March 4, 1913, and its bureaus and agencies specializing in labor were transferred to the new Department of Labor.

Chapter 1. Part I Introduction to Intellectual Property

Chapter 1. Part I Introduction to Intellectual Property

Federal Deposit Insurance Corporation	The Federal Deposit Insurance Corporation is a United States government corporation created by the Glass-Steagall Act of 1933. It provides deposit insurance, which guarantees the safety of deposits in member banks, currently up to $250,000 per depositor per bank. Funds in non-interest bearing transaction accounts are fully insured, with no limit, under the temporary Transaction Account Guarantee Program.
Congress	A Congress is a formal meeting of representatives from different countries (or by extension constituent states), or independent organizations (such as different trade unions.) The term Congress was chosen for the United States Congress to emphasize the status of each state represented there as a self-governing unit. Subsequently to the use of Congress by the US legislature, the term has been adopted by many states within unions, and by unitary nation-states in the Americas, to refer to their legislatures.
European Union	The European Union is an economic and political union of 27 member states, located primarily in Europe. It was established by the Treaty of Maastricht on 1 November 1993, upon the foundations of the pre-existing European Economic Community. With a population of almost 500 million, the European Union generates an estimated 30% share (US$18.4 trillion in 2008) of the nominal gross world product.
Madrid system for the international registration of marks	The Madrid system for the international registration of marks, also conveniently known as the Madrid system or simply Madrid, is the primary international system for facilitating the registration of trademarks in multiple jurisdictions around the world. The Madrid system provides a centrally administered system of obtaining a bundle of trademark registrations in separate jurisdictions. Registration through the Madrid system does not create an "international" registration, as in the case of the European CTM system, rather it creates a bundle of national rights, able to be administered centrally.
World Intellectual Property Organization	The World Intellectual Property Organization is one of the 16 specialized agencies of the United Nations. World Intellectual Property Organization was created in 1967 "to encourage creative activity, to promote the protection of intellectual property throughout the world". World Intellectual Property Organization currently has 184 member states, administers 24 international treaties, and is headquartered in Geneva, Switzerland.
General Agreement on Tariffs and Trade	The General Agreement on Tariffs and Trade was the outcome of the failure of negotiating governments to create the International Trade Organization (ITO.) GATT was formed in 1947 and lasted until 1994, when it was replaced by the World Trade Organization. The Bretton Woods Conference had introduced the idea for an organization to regulate trade as part of a larger plan for economic recovery after World War II.
North American Free Trade Agreement	The North American Free Trade Agreement is a trilateral trade bloc in North America created by the governments of the United States, Canada, and Mexico. The agreement creating the trade bloc came into force on January 1, 1994. It superseded the Canada-United States Free Trade Agreement between the U.S. and Canada.

Chapter 1. Part I Introduction to Intellectual Property

Chapter 1. Part I Introduction to Intellectual Property

Tariff	A Tariff is a duty imposed on goods when they are moved across a political boundary. They are usually associated with protectionism, the economic policy of restraining trade between nations. For political reasons, Tariff s are usually imposed on imported goods, although they may also be imposed on exported goods.

Chapter 2. Part II The Law of Trademarks

Collective mark	A collective trade mark or Collective mark is a trademark owned by an organisation (such as an association), whose members use them to identify themselves with a level of quality or accuracy, geographical origin, or other characteristics set by the organisation. Collective trade marks are exceptions to the underlying principle of trade marks in that most trade marks serve as "badges of origin" - they indicate the individual source of the goods or services. A collective trade mark, however, can be used by a variety of traders, rather than just one individual concern, provided that the trader belongs to the association.
Affidavit	An Affidavit is a formal sworn statement of fact, signed by the author, who is called the affiant or deponent, and witnessed as to the authenticity of the affiant"s signature by a taker of oaths, such as a notary public or commissioner of oaths. The name is Medieval Latin for he has declared upon oath. An Affidavit is a type of verified statement or showing, or in other words, it contains a verification, meaning it is under oath or penalty of perjury, and this serves as evidence to its veracity and is required for court proceedings.
Three-card Monte	Three-card Monte Three-card trick, Three-Way, Three-card shuffle, Menage-a-card, Triplets, Follow the lady, Find the lady or mark, is tricked into betting a sum of money that they can find the money card, for example the queen of hearts, among three face-down playing cards. In its full form, the Three-card Monte is an example of a classic short con in which the outside man pretends to conspire with the mark to cheat the inside man, while in fact conspiring with the inside man to cheat the mark. This confidence trick has a great deal in common with the shell game; they are the same except that cards are used instead of "shells".
Service mark	In some countries, notably the United States, a trademark used to identify a service rather than a product is called a Service mark or servicemark. When a Service mark is federally registered, the standard registration symbol Â® or "Reg U.S. Pat ' TM Off" may be used (the same symbol is used to mark registered trademarks.) Before it is registered, it is common practice (but has no legal standing) to use the Service mark symbol $^{\text{Service mark}}$ (a superscript Service mark.)
Trademark	A trademark or trade mark is a distinctive sign or indicator used by an individual, business organization and to distinguish its products or services from those of other entities. A trademark is designated by the following symbols: - â„¢ (for an unregistered trademark that is, a mark used to promote or brand goods); - â„ (for an unregistered service mark, that is, a mark used to promote or brand services); and - Â® (for a registered trademark) A trademark is a type of intellectual property, and typically a name, word, phrase, logo, symbol, design, image, or a combination of these elements. There is also a range of non-conventional trademark s comprising marks which do not fall into these standard categories. The owner of a registered trademark may commence legal proceedings for trademark infringement to prevent unauthorized use of that trademark

Chapter 2. Part II The Law of Trademarks

Chapter 2. Part II The Law of Trademarks

Job description	A Job description is a list of the general tasks and responsibilities of a position. Typically, it also includes to whom the position reports, specifications such as the qualifications needed by the person in the job, salary range for the position, etc. A Job description is usually developed by conducting a job analysis, which includes examining the tasks and sequences of tasks necessary to perform the job.
Certification mark	A Certification mark on a commercial product indicates five things: - The existence of a legal follow-up or product certification agreement between the manufacturer of a product and an organisation with national accreditation for both testing and certification, - Legal evidence that the product was successfully tested in accordance with a nationally accredited standard, - Legal assurance the accredited certification organization has ensured that the item that was successfully tested and is identical to that which is being offered for sale, - Legal assurance that the successful test has resulted in a certification listing, which is considered public information, which sets out the tolerances and conditions of use for the certified product, to enable compliance with the law through listing and approval use and compliance, - Legal assurance that the manufacturer is being regularly audited by the certification organisation to ensure the maintenance of the original process standard that was employed in the manufacture of the test specimen that passed the test. If the manufacturer should fail an audit, all product that was certified, including labels of stock on hand, on construction sites, with end-user customers and on distributor store shelves, can be mandated by the cirtification organisation in charge to be immediately removed, and can insist that all stakeholders be informed that the de-listed product certification is no longer eligible for use in field installations. On the part of the certifier, the label itself is a type of trademark whereby the listee, or manufacturer, uses the mark to indicate eligibility of the products for use in field installations in accordance with the requirements of the code, and/or the origin, material, mode of manufacture of products, mode of performance of services, quality, accuracy of other characteristics of products or services. Certification mark s differ from collective trade marks. The main difference is that collective trade marks may be used by particular members of the organization which owns them, while Certification mark s are the only evidence of the existence of follow-up agreements between manufacturers and nationally accredited testing and certification organisations. Certification organisations charge for the use of their labels and are thus always aware of exact production numbers.

Chapter 2. Part II The Law of Trademarks

Chapter 2. Part II The Law of Trademarks

The Commerce Clause	The Commerce Clause is an enumerated power listed in the United States Constitution (Article 1, Section 8, Clause 3.) The clause states that Congress has the power to regulate commerce with foreign nations, among the states, and with the Native American tribes. Courts and commentators have tended to discuss each of these three areas of commerce as a separate power granted to the Congress of the United States.
Abandonment	Abandonment, in law, is the relinquishment or renunciation of an interest, claim, privilege, possession or right, especially with the intent of never again resuming or reasserting it.
Common law	Common law refers to law and the corresponding legal system developed through decisions of courts and similar tribunals (called case law), rather than through legislative statutes or executive action.
	Common law is law created and refined by judges: a decision in a currently pending legal case depends on decisions in previous cases and affects the law to be applied in future cases. When there is no authoritative statement of the law, judges have the authority and duty to make law by creating precedent.
Principal Register	In United States trademark law, the Principal Register is the primary register of trademarks maintained by the United States Patent and Trademark Office. It is governed by Subchapter I of the Lanham Act.
	Having a mark registered under the Principal Register confers certain benefits on the holder of the mark.
Code of Federal Regulations	The Code of Federal Regulations is the codification of the general and permanent rules and regulations (sometimes called administrative law) published in the Federal Register by the executive departments and agencies of the Federal Government of the United States. The CFR is published by the Office of the Federal Register, an agency of the National Archives and Records Administration (NARA.)
	The CFR is divided into 50 titles that represent broad areas subject to Federal regulation.
Anticybersquatting Consumer Protection Act	The Anticybersquatting Consumer Protection Act, a United States federal law enacted in 1999, is part of A bill to amend the provisions of title 17, United States Code, and the Communications Act of 1934, relating to copyright licensing and carriage of broadcast signals by satellite . It makes people who register domain names that are either trademarks or individual"s names with the sole intent of selling the rights of the domain name to the trademark holder or individual for a profit liable to civil action. It was sponsored by Senator Trent Lott on November 17, 1999, and enacted on November 29 of the same year.
Consumer Protection	Consumer protection laws are designed to ensure fair competition and the free flow of truthful information in the marketplace. The laws are designed to prevent businesses that engage in fraud or specified unfair practices from gaining an advantage over competitors and may provide additional protection for the weak and unable to take care of themselves. Consumer protection laws are a form of government regulation which protects the interests of consumers.

Chapter 2. Part II The Law of Trademarks

Chapter 2. Part II The Law of Trademarks

Federal Trademark Dilution Act	The Federal Trademark Dilution Act of 1995 is a United States federal law which protects famous trademarks from uses that dilute their distinctiveness, even in the absence of any likelihood of confusion or competition. It went into effect on January 16, 1996. This act has been largely supplanted by the Trademark Dilution Revision Act of 2006 (TDRA), signed into law on October 6, 2006.
Intellectual Property	Intellectual property are legal property rights over creations of the mind, both artistic and commercial, and the corresponding fields of law. Under intellectual property law, owners are granted certain exclusive rights to a variety of intangible assets, such as musical, literary, and artistic works; ideas, discoveries and inventions; and words, phrases, symbols, and designs. Common types of intellectual property include copyrights, trademarks, patents, industrial design rights and trade secrets.
Madrid system for the international registration of marks	The Madrid system for the international registration of marks, also conveniently known as the Madrid system or simply Madrid, is the primary international system for facilitating the registration of trademarks in multiple jurisdictions around the world. The Madrid system provides a centrally administered system of obtaining a bundle of trademark registrations in separate jurisdictions. Registration through the Madrid system does not create an "international" registration, as in the case of the European CTM system, rather it creates a bundle of national rights, able to be administered centrally.
North American Free Trade Agreement	The North American Free Trade Agreement is a trilateral trade bloc in North America created by the governments of the United States, Canada, and Mexico. The agreement creating the trade bloc came into force on January 1, 1994. It superseded the Canada-United States Free Trade Agreement between the U.S. and Canada.
Trademark distinctiveness	Trademark distinctiveness is an important concept in the law governing trademarks and service marks. A trademark may be eligible for registration, or registrable, if amongst other things it performs the essential trademark function, and has distinctive character. Registrability can be understood as a continuum, with "inherently distinctive" marks at one end, "generic" and "descriptive" marks with no distinctive character at the other end, and "suggestive" and "arbitrary" marks lying between these two points.
Trade name	A Trade name is the name which a business trades under for commercial purposes, although its registered, legal name, used for contracts and other formal situations, may be another. Pharmaceuticals also have Trade name s, often dissimilar to their chemical names Trading names are sometimes registered as trademarks or are regarded as brands.
Disparagement	Disparagement, in United States trademark law, is a statutory cause of action that permits a party to petition the Trademark Trial and Appeal Board (TTAB) of the Patent and Trademark Office (PTO) to cancel a trademark registration that "may disparage or falsely suggest a connection with persons, living or dead, institutions, beliefs or bring them into contempt or disrepute." Unlike claims regarding the validity of the mark, a Disparagement claim can be brought "at any time," subject to equitable defenses such as laches.

Chapter 2. Part II The Law of Trademarks

Chapter 2. Part II The Law of Trademarks

	The TTAB has interpreted the Lanham Act to give broad standing to parties who claim they may be injured by a mark. In one case, the TTAB permitted two women to seek the cancellation of a chicken restaurant"s slogan, "Only a Breast in the Mouth is Better Than a Leg in the Hand." Other examples of trademarks that were refused or cancelled for Disparagement include a depiction of Buddha for beachwear, use of the name of a Muslim group that forbids smoking as a cigarette brand name, and an image consisting of a large "X" over the hammer and sickle national symbol of the Soviet Union.
Domain name	A Domain name is an identification label that defines a realm of administrative autonomy, authority, or control in the Internet, based on the Domain name System (Domain name S.) Domain name s are used in various networking contexts and application-specific naming and addressing purposes. They are organized in subordinate levels (subdomains) of the Domain name S root domain, which is nameless.
Patent	A patent is a set of exclusive rights granted by a state to an inventor or his assignee for a limited period of time in exchange for a disclosure of an invention. The procedure for granting patent s, the requirements placed on the patent ee and the extent of the exclusive rights vary widely between countries according to national laws and international agreements. Typically, however, a patent application must include one or more claims defining the invention which must be new, inventive, and useful or industrially applicable.
Supreme Court	A supreme court is in some jurisdictions the highest judicial body within that jurisdiction"s court system, whose rulings are not subject to further review by another court. The designations for such courts differ among jurisdictions. Courts of last resort typically function primarily as appellate courts, hearing appeals from the lower trial courts or intermediate-level appellate courts.
Trade dress	Trade dress is a legal term of art that generally refers to characteristics of the visual appearance of a product or its packaging (or even the design of a building) that signify the source of the product to consumers. Trade dress is a form of intellectual property. In the U.S., like trademarks, a product"s Trade dress is legally protected by the Lanham Act, the federal statute which regulates trademarks and Trade dress.
Appeal	In law, an appeal is a process for requesting a formal change to an official decision. The specific procedures for appeal ing, including even whether there is a right of appeal from a particular type of decision, can vary greatly from country to country. Even within a jurisdiction, the nature of an appeal can vary greatly depending on the type of case.

Chapter 2. Part II The Law of Trademarks

Chapter 2. Part II The Law of Trademarks

Trial	In law, a trial is when parties come together to a dispute present information (in the form of evidence) in a formal setting, usually a court, before a judge, jury in order to achieve a resolution to their dispute. - Where the trial is held before a group of members of the community, it is called a jury trial - Where the trial is held solely before a judge, it is called a bench trial Bench trial s involve fewer formalities, and are typically resolved faster. Furthermore, a favorable ruling for one party in a bench trial will frequently lead the other party to offer a settlement. Hearings before administrative bodies may have many of the features of a trial before a court, but are typically not referred to as trial s. An appellate proceeding is also generally not deemed a trial because such proceedings are usually restricted to review of the evidence presented before the trial court, and do not permit the introduction of new evidences. trial s can also be divided by the type of dispute at issue.
Due diligence	Due diligence is a term used for a number of concepts involving either the performance of an investigation of a business or person, or the performance of an act with a certain standard of care. It can be a legal obligation, but the term will more commonly apply to voluntary investigations. A common example of Due diligence in various industries is the process through which a potential acquirer evaluates a target company or its assets for acquisition.
Job interview	A Job interview is a process in which a potential employee is evaluated by an employer for prospective employment in their company, organization and was established in the late 16th century. A Job interview typically precedes the hiring decision, and is used to evaluate the candidate. The interview is usually preceded by the evaluation of submitted résumés from interested candidates, then selecting a small number of candidates for interviews.
Libel	In law, defamation, slander, and vilification) is the communication of a statement that makes a claim, expressly stated or implied to be factual, that may give an individual, business, product, group, government or nation a negative image. It is usually, but not always, a requirement that this claim be false and that the publication is communicated to someone other than the person defamed In common law jurisdictions, slander refers to a malicious, false and defamatory spoken statement or report, while Libel refers to any other form of communication such as written words or images.
Evaluation	Evaluation is systematic determination of merit, worth, and significance of something or someone using criteria against a set of standards. Evaluation often is used to characterize and appraise subjects of interest in a wide range of human enterprises, including the arts, criminal justice, foundations and non-profit organizations, government, health care, and other human services.

Chapter 2. Part II The Law of Trademarks

Chapter 2. Part II The Law of Trademarks

	Depending on the topic of interest, there are professional groups which look to the quality and rigor of the Evaluation process.
Good	A good is an object whose consumption increases the utility of the consumer, for which the quantity demanded exceeds the quantity supplied at zero price. Goods are usually modeled as having diminishing marginal utility. The first individual purchase has high utility; the second has less.
Goods and services	In economics, economic output is divided into physical goods and intangible services. Consumption of Goods and services is assumed to produce utility. It is often used when referring to a Goods and services Tax.
Deposit account	A Deposit account is a current account at a banking institution that allows money to be deposited and withdrawn by the account holder, with the transactions and resulting balance being recorded on the bank"s books. Some banks charge a fee for this service, while others may pay the customer interest on the funds deposited. Although restrictions placed on access depend upon the terms and conditions of the account and the provider, the account holder retains rights to have their funds repaid on demand.
Disclaimer	A disclaimer is generally any statement intended to specify or delimit the scope of rights and obligations that may be exercised and enforced by parties in a legally-recognized relationship. In contrast to other terms for legally operative language, the term disclaimer usually implies situations that involve some level of uncertainty, waiver, or risk. A disclaimer may specify mutually-agreed and privately-arranged terms and conditions as part of a contract; or may specify warnings or expectations to the general public (or some other class of persons) in order to fulfill a duty of care owed to prevent unreasonable risk of harm or injury.
Cease and Desist	A Cease and desist is an order or request to halt an activity, or else face legal action. The recipient of the cease-and-desist may be an individual or an organization.
Copyright	Copyright gives the creator of an original work exclusive right for a certain time period in relation to that work, including its publication, distribution and adaptation; after which time the work is said to enter the public domain. Copyright applies to any expressible form of an idea or information that is substantive and discrete and fixed in a medium. Some jurisdictions also recognize "moral rights" of the creator of a work, such as the right to be credited for the work.
License	The verb License or grant License means to give permission. The noun License refers to that permission as well as to the document memorializing that permission. License may be granted by a party to another party as an element of an agreement between those parties.

Chapter 2. Part II The Law of Trademarks

Chapter 2. Part II The Law of Trademarks

Security agreement	A security agreement is the contract that governs the relationship between the parties to a secured transaction (ie, the lender and the borrower A written security agreement needs a description of the collateral, must be authenticated by the borrower (ie, signed), and must use words showing an intent to create a security interest
Federal Rules of Civil Procedure	The Federal Rules of Civil Procedure are rules governing civil procedure in United States district (federal) courts, that is, court procedures for civil suits. The FRCP are promulgated by the United States Supreme Court pursuant to the Rules Enabling Act, and then approved by the United States Congress. The Court"s modifications to the rules are usually based on recommendations from the Judicial Conference of the United States, the federal judiciary"s internal policy-making body.
Petition	A petition is a request to change something, most commonly made to a government official or public entity. petition s to a deity are a form of prayer. In the colloquial sense, a petition is a document addressed to some official and signed by numerous individuals.
Trademark infringement	Trademark infringement is a violation of the exclusive rights attaching to a trademark without the authorization of the trademark owner or any licensees (provided that such authorization was within the scope of the license.) Infringement may occur when one party, the "infringer", uses a trademark which is identical or confusingly similar to a trademark owned by another party, in relation to products or services which are identical or similar to the products or services which the registration covers. An owner of a trademark may commence legal proceedings against a party which infringes its registration.
Defenses	In the field of criminal law there are a variety of conditions that will tend to negate elements of a crime (particularly the intent element), known as defenses. The label may be apt in jurisdictions where the accused may be assigned some burden before a tribunal. However, in many jurisdictions, the entire burden to prove a crime is on the government, which also must prove the absence of these defenses, where implicated.
Intent	Intent in law is the planning and desire to perform an act, to fail to do so (i.e. an omission) or to achieve a state of affairs in psychological view it may mean a different thing. In criminal law, for a given actus reus ("guilty act"), the required element to prove intent consists of showing mens rea (mental state, "guilty mind".) The requirements for the proof of intent in tort law are generally simpler than criminal law.
Infringement	Infringement, when used alone, has several possible meanings in the English language.

Chapter 2. Part II The Law of Trademarks

Chapter 2. Part II The Law of Trademarks

In a legal context, an infringement refers to the violation of a law or a right. This includes intellectual property infringements such as:

- copyright infringement
- patent infringement
- trademark infringement
- civel building infringement

Dispute

Controversy is a state of prolonged public dispute or debate usually concerning a matter of opinion. The term originates circa 1384 from Latin controversia, as a composite of controversus - "turned in an opposite direction," from contra - "against" - and vertere - to turn, or versus , hence, "to turn against."

Benford"s law of controversy, as expressed by science-fiction author Gregory Benford in 1980, states: "Passion is inversely proportional to the amount of real (true) information available." In other words, the more untruths the more controversy there is, and the more truths the less controversy there is.

A controversy is always the result of either ignorance (lack of sufficient true information), misinformation, misunderstandings, half-truths, distortions, bias or prejudice, deliberate lies or fabrications (disinformation), opposed underlying motives or purposes (sometimes masked or hidden), or a combination of these factors.

Litigation

The conduct of a lawsuit is called Litigation.

Rules of criminal or civil procedure govern the conduct of a lawsuit in the common law adversarial system of dispute resolution. Procedural rules are additionally constrained/informed by separate statutory laws, case law, and constitutional provisions that define the rights of the parties to a lawsuit , though the rules will generally reflect this legal context on their face.

International Trade

International trade is exchange of capital, goods, and services across international borders or territories. In most countries, it represents a significant share of gross domestic product (GDP.) While International trade has been present throughout much of history , its economic, social, and political importance has been on the rise in recent centuries.

International Trade Commission

The United States International Trade Commission is an independent, non-partisan, quasi-judicial, federal agency of the United States that provides trade expertise to both the legislative and executive branches. Further, the agency determines the impact of imports on U.S. industries and directs actions against certain unfair trade practices, such as dumping, patent, trademark, and copyright infringement.

The US International Trade Commission was established by the U.S. Congress in 1916 as the U.S. Tariff Commission (the Trade Act of 1974 changed its name to the U.S. International Trade Commission , the agency has broad investigative powers on matters of trade.

Chapter 2. Part II The Law of Trademarks

Chapter 2. Part II The Law of Trademarks

Tariff	A Tariff is a duty imposed on goods when they are moved across a political boundary. They are usually associated with protectionism, the economic policy of restraining trade between nations. For political reasons, Tariff s are usually imposed on imported goods, although they may also be imposed on exported goods.
Grey market	A Grey market is the trade of a commodity through distribution channels which, while legal, are unofficial, unauthorized, or unintended by the original manufacturer. In contrast, a black market is the trade of goods and services that are illegal in themselves and/or distributed through illegal channels, such as the selling of stolen goods, certain drugs or unregistered handguns. The two main types of Grey market are imported manufactured goods that would normally be unavailable or more expensive in a certain country and unissued securities that are not yet traded in official markets.
Import	An import is any good (e.g. a commodity) or service brought into one country from another country in a legitimate fashion, typically for use in trade.It is a good that is brought in from another country for sale. import goods or services are provided to domestic consumers by foreign producers. An import in the receiving country is an export to the sending country.
Doctrine of exhaustion	Under the Doctrine of exhaustion the first unrestricted sale of a patented item exhausts the patentee"s control over that particular item. It generally is asserted as an affirmative defense to charges of patent infringement, but less commonly is asserted affirmatively in a declaratory judgment action. In other words, it is a concept in intellectual property law whereby an intellectual property owner will lose or "exhaust" certain rights after the first use of the subject matter which is the subject of intellectual property rights.
Unfair competition	Unfair competition in commercial law can refer to any of various distinct areas of law which may give rise to distinct criminal offences and civil causes of action: - Matters pertaining to antitrust law, known in the European Union as competition law. - Unfair business practices such as fraud, misrepresentation, tortious interference, and unconscionable contracts and business practices. In the European Union, each member state must regulate unfair business practices in accordance with the principles laid down in the Unfair Commercial Practices Directive, subject to transitional periods. (.
Corporation	The institution most often referenced by the word "corporation" is a public or publicly traded corporation, the shares of which are traded on a public stock exchange (e.g., the New York Stock Exchange or Nasdaq in the United States) where shares of stock of corporations are bought and sold by and to the general public. Most of the largest businesses in the world are publicly traded corporations. However, the majority of corporations are said to be closely held, privately held or close corporations, meaning that no ready market exists for the trading of shares.

Chapter 2. Part II The Law of Trademarks

Chapter 2. Part II The Law of Trademarks

Federal Trade Commission	The Federal Trade Commission is an independent agency of the United States government, established in 1914 by the Federal Trade Commission Act. Its principal mission is the promotion of "consumer protection" and the elimination and prevention of what regulators perceive to be harmfully "anti-competitive" business practices, such as coercive monopoly. The Federal Trade Commission Act was one of President Wilson"s major acts against trusts.
Dispute Resolution	Dispute resolution is the process of resolving disputes between parties. Methods of Dispute resolution include: - lawsuits (litigation) - arbitration - collaborative law - mediation - conciliation - many types of negotiation - facilitation One could theoretically include violence or even war as part of this spectrum, but Dispute resolution practitioners do not usually do so; violence rarely ends disputes effectively, and indeed, often only escalates them. Some individuals, notably Joseph Stalin, have stated that all problems emanate from man, and absent man, no problems ensue. Hence, violence could theoretically end disputes, but alongside it, life.
Uniform Domain-Name Dispute-Resolution Policy	The Uniform Domain-Name Dispute-Resolution Policy is a process established by the Internet Corporation for Assigned Names and Numbers (ICANN) for the resolution of disputes regarding the registration of internet domain names. The UDRP currently applies to all .biz, .com, .info, .name, .net, and .org top-level domains, and some country code top-level domains. When a registrant chooses a domain name, the registrant must "represent and warrant," among other things, that registering the name "will not infringe upon or otherwise violate the rights of any third party," and agree to participate in an arbitration-like proceeding should any third party assert such a claim.
World Intellectual Property Organization	The World Intellectual Property Organization is one of the 16 specialized agencies of the United Nations. World Intellectual Property Organization was created in 1967 "to encourage creative activity, to promote the protection of intellectual property throughout the world". World Intellectual Property Organization currently has 184 member states, administers 24 international treaties, and is headquartered in Geneva, Switzerland.
First Amendment	The First Amendment to the United States Constitution is the part of the United States Bill of Rights that expressly prohibits the United States Congress from making laws "respecting an establishment of religion" or that prohibit the free exercise of religion, infringe the freedom of speech, infringe the freedom of the press, limit the right to peaceably assemble, or limit the right to petition the government for a redress of grievances.

Chapter 2. Part II The Law of Trademarks

Chapter 2. Part II The Law of Trademarks

	Although the First Amendment only explicitly applies to the Congress, the Supreme Court has interpreted it as applying to the executive and judicial branches. Additionally, in the 20th century, the Supreme Court held that the Due Process Clause of the Fourteenth Amendment applies the limitations of the First Amendment to each state, including any local government within a state.
Cyberspace	Cyberspace is the global domain of electromagnetics as accessed and exploited through electronic technology and the modulation of electromagnetic energy to achieve a wide range of communication and control system capabilities. The term is rooted in the science of cybernetics and Norbert Wiener"s pioneering work in electronic communication and control science, a forerunner to current information theory and computer science. Through its electromagnetic nature, Cyberspace integrates a number of capabilities and generates a virtual interactive experience accessed for the purpose of communication and control regardless of a geographic location.
Phishing	In the field of computer security, Phishing is the criminally fraudulent process of attempting to acquire sensitive information such as usernames, passwords and credit card details by masquerading as a trustworthy entity in an electronic communication. Communications purporting to be from popular social web sites, auction sites, online payment processors or IT Administrators are commonly used to lure the unsuspecting public. Phishing is typically carried out by e-mail or instant messaging, and it often directs users to enter details at a fake website whose look and feel are almost identical to the legitimate one.
Playboy Enterprises, Inc. v. Welles	Playboy Enterprises, Inc. v. Welles, 279 F.3d 796 (9th Cir. 2002), is an influential United States Circuit Court decision from the U.S. Court of Appeals for the 9th Circuit regarding nominative use of trademarks.
Complaint	In general use , a Complaint is an expression of displeasure, such as poor service at a store etc. In legal terminology, a Complaint is a formal legal document that sets out the basic facts and legal reasons that the filing party (the plaintiffs) believes are sufficient to support a claim against another person, persons, entity or entities (the defendants) that entitles the plaintiff(s) to a remedy (either money damages or injunctive relief.) For example, the Federal Rules of Civil Procedure that govern civil litigation in United States courts provide that a civil action is commenced with the filing or service of a pleading called a Complaint.
NAFTA	NAFTA-NAFTA is a trilateral trade bloc in North America created by the governments of the United States, Canada, and Mexico. The agreement creating the trade bloc came into force on January 1, 1994. It superseded the Canada-United States Free Trade Agreement between the U.S. and Canada.
Consideration	Consideration is a concept of legal value in contract law. It is a promised action, or omission of action, that the promisee did not already have a pre-existing duty to abide by. It can take the form of money, physical objects, services, or a forbearance of action.

Chapter 2. Part II The Law of Trademarks

Chapter 2. Part II The Law of Trademarks

European Union	The European Union is an economic and political union of 27 member states, located primarily in Europe. It was established by the Treaty of Maastricht on 1 November 1993, upon the foundations of the pre-existing European Economic Community. With a population of almost 500 million, the European Union generates an estimated 30% share (US$18.4 trillion in 2008) of the nominal gross world product.
General Agreement on Tariffs and Trade	The General Agreement on Tariffs and Trade was the outcome of the failure of negotiating governments to create the International Trade Organization (ITO.) GATT was formed in 1947 and lasted until 1994, when it was replaced by the World Trade Organization. The Bretton Woods Conference had introduced the idea for an organization to regulate trade as part of a larger plan for economic recovery after World War II.
World Trade Organization	The World Trade Organization is an important selective, mainly private, international organization designed by its founders to supervise and liberalize international trade. The organization officially commenced on 1 January 1995, under the Marrakesh Agreement, succeding the 1947 General Agreement on Tariffs and Trade (GATT.)
	The World Trade Organization deals with regulation of trade between participating countries; it provides a framework for negotiating and formalising trade agreements, and a dispute resolution process aimed at enforcing participants" adherence to World Trade Organization agreements which are signed by representatives of member governments and ratified by their parliaments.

Chapter 2. Part II The Law of Trademarks

Chapter 3. Part III The Law of Copyrights

Constitution	A Constitution is set of rules for government -- often codified as a written document -- that establishes principles of an autonomous political entity. In the case of countries, this term refers specifically to a national Constitution defining the fundamental political principles, and establishing the structure, procedures, powers and duties, of a government. By limiting the government"s own reach, most Constitution s guarantee certain rights to the people.
Copyright	Copyright gives the creator of an original work exclusive right for a certain time period in relation to that work, including its publication, distribution and adaptation; after which time the work is said to enter the public domain. Copyright applies to any expressible form of an idea or information that is substantive and discrete and fixed in a medium. Some jurisdictions also recognize "moral rights" of the creator of a work, such as the right to be credited for the work.
Statute	A statute is a formal written enactment of a legislative authority that governs a country, state, city, or county. Typically, statute s command or prohibit something, or declare policy. The word is often used to distinguish law made by legislative bodies from case law and the regulations issued by Government agencies.
Congress	A Congress is a formal meeting of representatives from different countries (or by extension constituent states), or independent organizations (such as different trade unions.) The term Congress was chosen for the United States Congress to emphasize the status of each state represented there as a self-governing unit. Subsequently to the use of Congress by the US legislature, the term has been adopted by many states within unions, and by unitary nation-states in the Americas, to refer to their legislatures.
Copyright Office	The United States Copyright Office, a part of the Library of Congress, is the official U.S. government body that maintains records of copyright registration in the United States. It is used by copyright title searchers who are attempting to clear a chain of title for copyrighted works. The head of the Copyright Office is called the Register of Copyrights.
Copyright Term Extension Act	The Copyright Term Extension Act of 1998 extended copyright terms in the United States by 20 years. Since the Copyright Act of 1976, copyright would last for the life of the author plus 50 years, or 75 years for a work of corporate authorship. The Act extended these terms to life of the author plus 70 years and for works of corporate authorship to 120 years after creation or 95 years after publication, whichever endpoint is earlier.
Digital Millennium Copyright Act	The Digital Millennium Copyright Act is a United States copyright law that implements two 1996 treaties of the World Intellectual Property Organization (WIPO.) It criminalizes production and dissemination of technology, devices, or services intended to circumvent measures (commonly known as Digital Rights Management or DRM) that control access to copyrighted works. It also criminalizes the act of circumventing an access control, whether or not there is actual infringement of copyright itself.

Chapter 3. Part III The Law of Copyrights

Chapter 3. Part III The Law of Copyrights

Sonny Bono Act	This law Sonny Bono Act effectively "froze" the advancement date of the public domain in the United States for works covered by the older fixed term copyright rules. Under this Act, additional works made in 1923 or afterwards that were still copyrighted in 1998 will not enter the public domain until 2019 or afterward unless the owner of the copyright releases them into the public domain prior to that or if the copyright gets extended again. Unlike copyright extension legislation in the European Union, the Sonny Bono Act did not revive copyrights that had already expired.
United States Copyright Office	The United States Copyright Office, a part of the Library of Congress, is the official U.S. government body that maintains records of copyright registration in the United States. It is used by copyright title searchers who are attempting to clear a chain of title for copyrighted works. The head of the Copyright Office is called the Register of Copyrights.
Mergers	The phrase Mergers and acquisitions refers to the aspect of corporate strategy, corporate finance and management dealing with the buying, selling and combining of different companies that can aid, finance, or help a growing company in a given industry grow rapidly without having to create another business entity. An acquisition, also known as a takeover or a buyout, is the buying of one company (the "target") by another. An acquisition may be friendly or hostile.
Procter ' Gamble	Procter is a surname, and may also refer to: - Bryan Waller Procter (pseud. Barry Cornwall), English poet - Goodwin Procter, American law firm - Procter ' Gamble, consumer products multinational
Public domain	The Public domain is a range of abstract materials--commonly referred to as intellectual property--which are not owned or controlled by anyone. The term indicates that these materials are therefore "public property", and available for anyone to use for any purpose. The Public domain can be defined in contrast to several forms of intellectual property; the Public domain in contrast to copyrighted works is different from the Public domain in contrast to trademarks or patented works.
Independent contractor	An Independent contractor is a natural person, business, or corporation which provides goods or services to another entity under terms specified in a contract or within a verbal agreement. Unlike an employee, an Independent contractor does not work regularly for an employer but works as and when required, during which time she or he may be subject to the Law of Agency. Independent contractor s are usually paid on a freelance basis.
Derivative work	A derivative work pertaining to copyright law, is an expressive creation that includes major, copyright-protected elements of an original, previously created first work. In the United States, the Copyright Act defines "derivative work" in 17 U.S.C. § 101:

Chapter 3. Part III The Law of Copyrights

	A "derivative work" is a work based upon one or more preexisting works, such as a translation, musical arrangement, dramatization, fictionalization, motion picture version, sound recording, art reproduction, abridgment, condensation, or any other form in which a work may be recast, transformed, or adapted.
Tort	Tort law is a body of law that addresses, and provides remedies for, civil wrongs not arising out of contractual obligations. A person who suffers legal damages may be able to use Tort law to receive compensation from someone who is legally responsible, or "liable," for those injuries. Generally speaking, Tort law defines what constitutes a legal injury and establishes the circumstances under which one person may be held liable for another"s injury.
Doctrine of exhaustion	Under the Doctrine of exhaustion the first unrestricted sale of a patented item exhausts the patentee"s control over that particular item. It generally is asserted as an affirmative defense to charges of patent infringement, but less commonly is asserted affirmatively in a declaratory judgment action. In other words, it is a concept in intellectual property law whereby an intellectual property owner will lose or "exhaust" certain rights after the first use of the subject matter which is the subject of intellectual property rights.
Supreme Court	A supreme court is in some jurisdictions the highest judicial body within that jurisdiction"s court system, whose rulings are not subject to further review by another court. The designations for such courts differ among jurisdictions. Courts of last resort typically function primarily as appellate courts, hearing appeals from the lower trial courts or intermediate-level appellate courts.
Reseller	A reseller is a company or individual that purchases goods or services with the intention of reselling them rather than consuming or using them. This is usually done for profit (but could be resold at a loss.) One example can be found in the industry of telecommunications, where companies buy excess amounts of transmission capacity or call time from other carriers and resell it to smaller carriers.
Attribution	In the arts and antiques, Attribution is the judgment by experts as to the authorship, date, or other aspect of the origin of a work of art or cultural artifact. Works "attributed" to an artist are more firmly believed to be theirs than those "ascribed".

Chapter 3. Part III The Law of Copyrights

Chapter 3. Part III The Law of Copyrights

Attribution can also mean:

- Attribution, a concept in copyright law requiring an author to be credited
- Journalism sourcing (or Attribution), a journalistic practice of attributing information to its source
- Attribution (psychology), a concept in psychology whereby people attribute traits and causes to things they observe
- Performance Attribution, a technique in quantitative finance for explaining the active performance of a portfolio

Fair use	Fair use is a doctrine in United States copyright law that allows limited use of copyrighted material without requiring permission from the rights holders, such as use for scholarship or review. It provides for the legal, non-licensed citation or incorporation of copyrighted material in another author"s work under a four-factor balancing test. The term "Fair use" originated in the United States, but has been added to Israeli law as well; a similar principle, fair dealing, exists in some other common law jurisdictions.
Limitations	A statute of limitations is a statute in a common law legal system that sets forth the maximum period of time, after certain events, that legal proceedings based on those events may be initiated. In civil law systems, similar provisions are usually part of the civil code or criminal code and are often known collectively as "periods of prescription" or "prescriptive periods."
	A common law legal system might have a statute limiting the time for prosecution of crimes called misdemeanors to two years after the offense occurred. In that statute, if a person is discovered to have committed a misdemeanor three years ago, the time has expired for the prosecution of the misdemeanor.
Compulsory license	In a compulsory license, a government forces the holder of a patent, copyright, or other exclusive right to grant use to the state or others. Usually, the holder does receive some royalties, either set by law or determined through some form of arbitration.
	A compulsory copyright license is an exception to copyright law that is usually philosophically justified as an attempt by the government to correct a market failure.
Intent	Intent in law is the planning and desire to perform an act, to fail to do so (i.e. an omission) or to achieve a state of affairs in psychological view it may mean a different thing.
	In criminal law, for a given actus reus ("guilty act"), the required element to prove intent consists of showing mens rea (mental state, "guilty mind".)
	The requirements for the proof of intent in tort law are generally simpler than criminal law.

Chapter 3. Part III The Law of Copyrights

Chapter 3. Part III The Law of Copyrights

Employment	Employment is a contract between two parties, one being the employer and the other being the employee. An employee may be defined as: "A person in the service of another under any contract of hire, express or implied, oral or written, where the employer has the power or right to control and direct the employee in the material details of how the work is to be performed." Black"s Law Dictionary page 471 (5th ed. 1979.)
Scope of employment	Scope of employment is the legal consideration of the various activities which may occur in the performance of a person"s job, especially those acts which are reasonable relative to the job description and foreseeable by the employer. Key examples of this consideration under US law can include tort liability of the employer due to a duty to supervise or control the employee. If a security guard harms a customer in a retail store, a court may consider if the employee"s harmful acts were foreseeable by the employer to the point that the employer should have instituted reasonable precautions to prevent the resulting harm.
Eldred v. Ashcroft	Eldred v. Ashcroft, 537 U.S. 186 (2003) was a court case in the United States challenging the constitutionality of the 1998 Sonny Bono Copyright Term Extension Act (CTEA.) Oral argument was heard on October 9, 2002, and on January 15, 2003, the court held the CTEA constitutional by a 7-2 decision. The Sonny Bono Copyright Term Extension Act (or CTEA) extended existing copyright terms by an additional 20 years from the terms set by the Copyright Act of 1976.
Deposit account	A Deposit account is a current account at a banking institution that allows money to be deposited and withdrawn by the account holder, with the transactions and resulting balance being recorded on the bank"s books. Some banks charge a fee for this service, while others may pay the customer interest on the funds deposited. Although restrictions placed on access depend upon the terms and conditions of the account and the provider, the account holder retains rights to have their funds repaid on demand.
Estoppel	Estoppel is a legal doctrine at common law, where a party is barred from claiming or denying an argument on an equitable ground. Estoppel complements the requirement of consideration in contract law. In general, Estoppel protects an aggrieved party, if the counter-party induced an expectation from the aggrieved party, and the aggrieved party reasonably relied on the expectation and would suffer detriment if the expectation is not met.
Due diligence	Due diligence is a term used for a number of concepts involving either the performance of an investigation of a business or person, or the performance of an act with a certain standard of care. It can be a legal obligation, but the term will more commonly apply to voluntary investigations. A common example of Due diligence in various industries is the process through which a potential acquirer evaluates a target company or its assets for acquisition.
Berne Convention Implementation Act	The Berne Convention Implementation Act of 1988 is a copyright act that came into force in the United States on March 1, 1989, making it a party to the Berne Convention for the Protection of Literary and Artistic Works.

Chapter 3. Part III The Law of Copyrights

Chapter 3. Part III The Law of Copyrights

The United States refused initially (that is, for 102 years from 1886 to 1988) to join the Berne Convention. There were some practical, justifiable reasons.

Infringement

Infringement, when used alone, has several possible meanings in the English language. In a legal context, an infringement refers to the violation of a law or a right. This includes intellectual property infringements such as:

- copyright infringement
- patent infringement
- trademark infringement
- civel building infringement

Copyright Infringement

Copyright infringement is the unauthorized use of material that is covered by copyright law, in a manner that violates one of the copyright owner"s exclusive rights, such as the right to reproduce or perform the copyrighted work, or to make derivative works.

For electronic and audio-visual media, unauthorized reproduction and distribution is occasionally referred to as piracy . The practice of labeling the act of infringement as "piracy" actually predates copyright itself.

Register of Copyrights

The Register of Copyrights is the director of the United States Copyright Office within the Library of Congress, as provided by 17 U.S.C. Â§ 701. The Office has been headed by a Register since 1897; as of 2008, the current Register is Marybeth Peters, the eleventh appointed Register and the fourteenth individual to serve in this position.

Defenses

In the field of criminal law there are a variety of conditions that will tend to negate elements of a crime (particularly the intent element), known as defenses. The label may be apt in jurisdictions where the accused may be assigned some burden before a tribunal. However, in many jurisdictions, the entire burden to prove a crime is on the government, which also must prove the absence of these defenses, where implicated.

Market

A market is any one of a variety of different systems, institutions, procedures, social relations and infrastructures whereby persons trade, and goods and services are exchanged, forming part of the economy. It is an arrangement that allows buyers and sellers to exchange things. market s vary in size, range, geographic scale, location, types and variety of human communities, as well as the types of goods and services traded.

Chapter 3. Part III The Law of Copyrights

Chapter 3. Part III The Law of Copyrights

Feist Publications, Inc., v. Rural Telephone Service Co.	Feist Publications, Inc., v. Rural Telephone Service Co., 499 U.S. 340 (1991), commonly called just Feist v. Rural, was a United States Supreme Court case in which Feist had copied information from Rural"s telephone listings to include in its own, after Rural had refused to license the information. Rural had sued for copyright infringement. The Court ruled that information contained in Rural"s phone directory was not copyrightable, and that therefore no infringement existed.
Extortion	"Extortion", outwresting property or services from a person, entity through coercion. Refraining from doing harm is sometimes euphemistically called protection. Extortion is commonly practiced by organized crime groups.
De minimis	De minimis is a Latin expression meaning about minimal things, normally in the phrases de minimis non curat praetor or de minimis non curat lex, meaning that the law is not interested in trivial matters. In a more formal legal sense "de minimis non curat lex" means something that is unworthy of the law"s attention. In risk assessment it refers to a level of risk that is too small to be concerned with.
Statute of limitations	A statute of limitations is a statute in a common law legal system that sets forth the maximum period of time, after certain events, that legal proceedings based on those events may be initiated. In civil law systems, similar provisions are usually part of the civil code or criminal code and are often known collectively as "periods of prescription" or "prescriptive periods." A common law legal system might have a statute limiting the time for prosecution of crimes called misdemeanors to two years after the offense occurred. In that statute, if a person is discovered to have committed a misdemeanor three years ago, the time has expired for the prosecution of the misdemeanor.
Appeal	In law, an appeal is a process for requesting a formal change to an official decision. The specific procedures for appeal ing, including even whether there is a right of appeal from a particular type of decision, can vary greatly from country to country. Even within a jurisdiction, the nature of an appeal can vary greatly depending on the type of case.
Federal Rules of Civil Procedure	The Federal Rules of Civil Procedure are rules governing civil procedure in United States district (federal) courts, that is, court procedures for civil suits. The FRCP are promulgated by the United States Supreme Court pursuant to the Rules Enabling Act, and then approved by the United States Congress. The Court"s modifications to the rules are usually based on recommendations from the Judicial Conference of the United States, the federal judiciary"s internal policy-making body.
International Trade	International trade is exchange of capital, goods, and services across international borders or territories. In most countries, it represents a significant share of gross domestic product (GDP.) While International trade has been present throughout much of history , its economic, social, and political importance has been on the rise in recent centuries.

Chapter 3. Part III The Law of Copyrights

Chapter 3. Part III The Law of Copyrights

International Trade Commission	The United States International Trade Commission is an independent, non-partisan, quasi-judicial, federal agency of the United States that provides trade expertise to both the legislative and executive branches. Further, the agency determines the impact of imports on U.S. industries and directs actions against certain unfair trade practices, such as dumping, patent, trademark, and copyright infringement. The US International Trade Commission was established by the U.S. Congress in 1916 as the U.S. Tariff Commission (the Trade Act of 1974 changed its name to the U.S. International Trade Commission , the agency has broad investigative powers on matters of trade.
Compensatory damages	Compensatory damages are paid to compensate the claimant for loss, injury, or harm suffered by another"s breach of duty. On a breach of contract by a defendant, a court generally awards the sum which would restore the injured party to the economic position that he or she expected from performance of the promise or promises . When it is either not possible or desirable to award damages measured in that way, a court may award money damages designed to restore the injured party to the economic position that he or she had occupied at the time the contract was entered, or designed to prevent the breaching party from being unjustly enriched
No Electronic Theft Act	The United States No Electronic Theft Act, a federal law passed in 1997, provides for criminal prosecution of individuals who engage in copyright infringement, even when there is no monetary profit or commercial benefit from the infringement. Maximum penalties can be five years in prison and up to $250,000 in fines. The NET Act also raised statutory damages by 50%.
Trust	In common law legal systems, a trust is an arrangement whereby property (including real, tangible and intangible) is managed by one person (or persons, or organizations) for the benefit of another. A trust is created by a settlor, who entrusts some or all of his or her property to people of his choice (the trustees.) The trustees hold legal title to the trust property (or trust corpus), but they are obliged to hold the property for the benefit of one or more individuals or organizations (the beneficiary, a.k.a. cestui que use or cestui que trust), usually specified by the settlor, who hold equitable title.
Object code	An object file format is a computer file format used for the storage of object code and related data typically produced by a compiler or assembler. There are many different object file formats; originally each type of computer had its own unique format, but with the advent of Unix and other portable operating systems, some formats, such as COFF and ELF, have been defined and used on different kinds of systems. It is common for the same file format to be used both as linker input and output, and thus as the library and executable file format.

Chapter 3. Part III The Law of Copyrights

Chapter 3. Part III The Law of Copyrights

Reverse engineering	Reverse engineering is the process of discovering the technological principles of a device, object or system through analysis of its structure, function and operation. It often involves taking something (e.g., a mechanical device, electronic component, or software program) apart and analyzing its workings in detail to be used in maintenance, or to try to make a new device or program that does the same thing without copying anything from the original. reverse engineering has its origins in the analysis of hardware for commercial or military advantage .
Clickwrap	A clickwrap agreement is a common type of agreement Such forms of agreement are mostly found on the Internet, as part of the installation process of many software packages, or in other circumstances where agreement is sought using electronic media. The name "clickwrap" came from the use of "shrink wrap contracts" commonly used in boxed software purchases, which "contain a notice that by tearing open the shrinkwrap, the user assents to the software terms enclosed within".
ProCD, Inc. v. Zeidenberg	ProCD, Inc. v. Zeidenberg, 86 F.3d 1447 (7th Cir., 1996), is a United States contract case involving a "shrink wrap license". The issue presented to the court was whether a shrink wrap license was valid and enforceable.
Cyberspace	Cyberspace is the global domain of electromagnetics as accessed and exploited through electronic technology and the modulation of electromagnetic energy to achieve a wide range of communication and control system capabilities. The term is rooted in the science of cybernetics and Norbert Wiener"s pioneering work in electronic communication and control science, a forerunner to current information theory and computer science. Through its electromagnetic nature, Cyberspace integrates a number of capabilities and generates a virtual interactive experience accessed for the purpose of communication and control regardless of a geographic location.
Broadcast flag	A Broadcast flag is a set of status bits (or a "flag") sent in the data stream of a digital television program that indicates whether or not the data stream can be recorded, or if there are any restrictions on recorded content. Possible restrictions include the inability to save an unencrypted digital program to a hard disk or other non-volatile storage, inability to make secondary copies of recorded content (in order to share or archive), forceful reduction of quality when recording (such as reducing high-definition video to the resolution of standard TVs), and inability to skip over commercials. In the United States, new television receivers using the ATSC standard were supposed to incorporate this functionality by July 1, 2005.

Chapter 3. Part III The Law of Copyrights

Chapter 3. Part III The Law of Copyrights

Digital rights management	Digital rights management is a generic term that refers to access control technologies that can be used by hardware manufacturers, publishers, copyright holders and individuals to try to impose limitations on the usage of digital content and devices. The term is used to describe any technology which makes the unauthorized use of such digital content and devices technically formidable, but generally doesn"t include other forms of copy protection which can be circumvented without modifying the file or device, such as serial numbers or keyfiles. It can also refer to restrictions associated with specific instances of digital works or devices.
First Amendment	The First Amendment to the United States Constitution is the part of the United States Bill of Rights that expressly prohibits the United States Congress from making laws "respecting an establishment of religion" or that prohibit the free exercise of religion, infringe the freedom of speech, infringe the freedom of the press, limit the right to peaceably assemble, or limit the right to petition the government for a redress of grievances.
	Although the First Amendment only explicitly applies to the Congress, the Supreme Court has interpreted it as applying to the executive and judicial branches. Additionally, in the 20th century, the Supreme Court held that the Due Process Clause of the Fourteenth Amendment applies the limitations of the First Amendment to each state, including any local government within a state.
Service provider	A service provider is an entity that provides services to other entities. Usually this refers to a business that provides subscription or web service to other businesses or individuals. Examples of these services include Internet access, Mobile phone operator, and web application hosting.
Intellectual Property	Intellectual property are legal property rights over creations of the mind, both artistic and commercial, and the corresponding fields of law. Under intellectual property law, owners are granted certain exclusive rights to a variety of intangible assets, such as musical, literary, and artistic works; ideas, discoveries and inventions; and words, phrases, symbols, and designs. Common types of intellectual property include copyrights, trademarks, patents, industrial design rights and trade secrets.
Napster	Napster was an online music file sharing service created by Shawn Fanning while he was attending Northeastern University in Boston and operating between June 1999 and July 2001. Its technology allowed people to easily copy and distribute MP3 files among each other, bypassing the established market for such songs and thus leading to the music industry"s accusations of massive copyright violations. Although the original service was shut down by court order, it paved the way for decentralized peer-to-peer file-distribution programs, which have been much harder to control.
Peer-to-peer	A Peer-to-peer computer network uses diverse connectivity between participants in a network and the cumulative bandwidth of network participants rather than conventional centralized resources where a relatively low number of servers provide the core value to a service or application.

Chapter 3. Part III The Law of Copyrights

Chapter 3. Part III The Law of Copyrights

	P2P networks are typically used for connecting nodes via largely ad hoc connections. Such networks are useful for many purposes.
Uniform Computer Information Transactions Act	The United States Uniform Computer Information Transactions Act is a proposed law to create a clear and uniform set of rules to govern such areas as software licensing, online access, and other transactions in computer information. It is intended to bring the same uniformity and certainty to the rules that apply to information technology transactions that the Uniform Commercial Code does for the sale of goods. In particular, Uniform Computer Information Transactions Act attempts to clarify and/or codify rules regarding fair use, reverse engineering, consumer protection and warranties, shrinkwrap licenses, and their duration as well as the transferability of licenses.
World Intellectual Property Organization	The World Intellectual Property Organization is one of the 16 specialized agencies of the United Nations. World Intellectual Property Organization was created in 1967 "to encourage creative activity, to promote the protection of intellectual property throughout the world". World Intellectual Property Organization currently has 184 member states, administers 24 international treaties, and is headquartered in Geneva, Switzerland.
WIPO Copyright Treaty	The World Intellectual Property Organization Copyright Treaty, abbreviated as the WIPO Copyright Treaty, is an international treaty on copyright law adopted by the member states of the World Intellectual Property Organization (WIPO) in 1996. It provides additional protections for copyright deemed necessary due to advances in information technology since the formation of previous copyright treaties before it. There have been a variety of criticisms of this treaty, including that it is overbroad (for example in its prohibition of circumvention of technical protection measures, even where such circumvention is used in the pursuit of legal and fair use rights) and that it applies a "one size fits all" standard to all signatory countries despite widely differing stages of economic development and knowledge industry.
WIPO Performances and Phonograms Treaty	The WIPO Performances and Phonograms Treaty is an international treaty signed by the member states of the World Intellectual Property Organization was adopted in Geneva on December 20, 1996. The Digital Millennium Copyright Act is the United States"s implementation of the treaty
General Agreement on Tariffs and Trade	The General Agreement on Tariffs and Trade was the outcome of the failure of negotiating governments to create the International Trade Organization (ITO.) GATT was formed in 1947 and lasted until 1994, when it was replaced by the World Trade Organization. The Bretton Woods Conference had introduced the idea for an organization to regulate trade as part of a larger plan for economic recovery after World War II.
Tariff	A Tariff is a duty imposed on goods when they are moved across a political boundary. They are usually associated with protectionism, the economic policy of restraining trade between nations. For political reasons, Tariff s are usually imposed on imported goods, although they may also be imposed on exported goods.

Chapter 3. Part III The Law of Copyrights

Chapter 3. Part III The Law of Copyrights

National treatment	National treatment is a principle in customary international law vital to many treaty regimes. It essentially means treating foreigners and locals equally. Under national treatment, if a state grants a particular right, benefit or privilege to its own citizens, it must also grant those advantages to the citizens of other states while they are in that country.
World Trade Organization	The World Trade Organization is an important selective, mainly private, international organization designed by its founders to supervise and liberalize international trade. The organization officially commenced on 1 January 1995, under the Marrakesh Agreement, succeeding the 1947 General Agreement on Tariffs and Trade (GATT.)
	The World Trade Organization deals with regulation of trade between participating countries; it provides a framework for negotiating and formalising trade agreements, and a dispute resolution process aimed at enforcing participants" adherence to World Trade Organization agreements which are signed by representatives of member governments and ratified by their parliaments.
Grey market	A Grey market is the trade of a commodity through distribution channels which, while legal, are unofficial, unauthorized, or unintended by the original manufacturer. In contrast, a black market is the trade of goods and services that are illegal in themselves and/or distributed through illegal channels, such as the selling of stolen goods, certain drugs or unregistered handguns.
	The two main types of Grey market are imported manufactured goods that would normally be unavailable or more expensive in a certain country and unissued securities that are not yet traded in official markets.
Good	A good is an object whose consumption increases the utility of the consumer, for which the quantity demanded exceeds the quantity supplied at zero price. Goods are usually modeled as having diminishing marginal utility. The first individual purchase has high utility; the second has less.

Chapter 3. Part III The Law of Copyrights

Chapter 4. Part IV The Law of Patents

Patent	A patent is a set of exclusive rights granted by a state to an inventor or his assignee for a limited period of time in exchange for a disclosure of an invention.
	The procedure for granting patent s, the requirements placed on the patent ee and the extent of the exclusive rights vary widely between countries according to national laws and international agreements. Typically, however, a patent application must include one or more claims defining the invention which must be new, inventive, and useful or industrially applicable.
Trademark	A trademark or trade mark is a distinctive sign or indicator used by an individual, business organization and to distinguish its products or services from those of other entities.
	A trademark is designated by the following symbols: • â„¢ (for an unregistered trademark that is, a mark used to promote or brand goods); • â„ (for an unregistered service mark, that is, a mark used to promote or brand services); and • Â® (for a registered trademark)
	A trademark is a type of intellectual property, and typically a name, word, phrase, logo, symbol, design, image, or a combination of these elements. There is also a range of non-conventional trademark s comprising marks which do not fall into these standard categories.
	The owner of a registered trademark may commence legal proceedings for trademark infringement to prevent unauthorized use of that trademark
American Inventors Protection Act	The American Inventors Protection Act is a United States federal law enacted on November 29, 1999 as Public Law 106-113. In 2002, the Intellectual Property and High Technology Technical Amendments Act of 2002, Public Law 107-273, amended American Inventors Protection Act.
	American Inventors Protection Act contains significant changes to American Patent Law.
Constitution	A Constitution is set of rules for government -- often codified as a written document -- that establishes principles of an autonomous political entity. In the case of countries, this term refers specifically to a national Constitution defining the fundamental political principles, and establishing the structure, procedures, powers and duties, of a government. By limiting the government"s own reach, most Constitution s guarantee certain rights to the people.
United States Code	The United States Code is a compilation and codification of the general and permanent federal law of the United States. It contains 50 titles and is published every six years by the Office of the Law Revision Counsel of the US House of Representatives.
	The official text of an Act of Congress is that of the "enrolled bill" (traditionally printed on parchment) presented to the President for his signature or disapproval.
Federal law	Federal law is the body of law created by the federal government of a country. A federal government is formed when a group of political units, such as states or provinces join together in a federation, surrendering their individual sovereignty and many powers to the central government while retaining or reserving other limited powers. As a result, two or more levels of government exist within an established geographic territory.

Chapter 4. Part IV The Law of Patents

Chapter 4. Part IV The Law of Patents

Appeal	In law, an appeal is a process for requesting a formal change to an official decision.
	The specific procedures for appeal ing, including even whether there is a right of appeal from a particular type of decision, can vary greatly from country to country. Even within a jurisdiction, the nature of an appeal can vary greatly depending on the type of case.
United States Patent and Trademark Office	The United States Patent and Trademark Office is an agency in the United States Department of Commerce that issues patents to inventors and businesses for their inventions, and trademark registration for product and intellectual property identification.
	The USPTO is currently based in Alexandria, Virginia, after a 2006 move from the Crystal City area of Arlington, Virginia. The offices under Patents and the Chief Information Officer that remained just outside the southern end of Crystal City completed moving to Randolph Square, a brand new building in Shirlington Village, on 27 April 2009.
Design patent	In the United States, a Design patent is a patent granted on the ornamental design of a functional item. Design patent s are a type of industrial design right. Ornamental designs of jewelry, furniture, beverage containers (see Fig.
Utility	In economics, utility is a measure of the relative satisfaction from consumption of various goods and services. Given this measure, one may speak meaningfully of increasing or decreasing utility, and thereby explain economic behavior in terms of attempts to increase one"s utility. For illustrative purposes, changes in utility are sometimes expressed in units called utils.
Abandonment	Abandonment, in law, is the relinquishment or renunciation of an interest, claim, privilege, possession or right, especially with the intent of never again resuming or reasserting it.
Prior art	Prior art, in most systems of patent law, constitutes all information that has been made available to the public in any form before a given date that might be relevant to a patent"s claims of originality. If an invention has been described in Prior art, a patent on that invention is not valid.
	Information kept secret, for instance, as a trade secret, is not usually Prior art, provided that employees and others with access to the information are under a non-disclosure obligation.
Consideration	Consideration is a concept of legal value in contract law. It is a promised action, or omission of action, that the promisee did not already have a pre-existing duty to abide by. It can take the form of money, physical objects, services, or a forbearance of action.
Diamond v. Diehr	Diamond v. Diehr, 450 U.S. 175 (1981), was a 1981 U.S. Supreme Court decision which held that the execution of a physical process, controlled by running a computer program was patentable. The high court reiterated its earlier holdings that software algorithms could not be patented, but it held that the mere presence of a software element did not make an otherwise patent-eligible machine or process un-patentable. Diehr was the third member of a trilogy of Supreme Court decisions on the patent-eligibility of computer software related inventions.

Chapter 4. Part IV The Law of Patents

Chapter 4. Part IV The Law of Patents

Import	An import is any good (e.g. a commodity) or service brought into one country from another country in a legitimate fashion, typically for use in trade. It is a good that is brought in from another country for sale. import goods or services are provided to domestic consumers by foreign producers. An import in the receiving country is an export to the sending country.
Disclaimer	A disclaimer is generally any statement intended to specify or delimit the scope of rights and obligations that may be exercised and enforced by parties in a legally-recognized relationship. In contrast to other terms for legally operative language, the term disclaimer usually implies situations that involve some level of uncertainty, waiver, or risk. A disclaimer may specify mutually-agreed and privately-arranged terms and conditions as part of a contract; or may specify warnings or expectations to the general public (or some other class of persons) in order to fulfill a duty of care owed to prevent unreasonable risk of harm or injury.
Limitations	A statute of limitations is a statute in a common law legal system that sets forth the maximum period of time, after certain events, that legal proceedings based on those events may be initiated. In civil law systems, similar provisions are usually part of the civil code or criminal code and are often known collectively as "periods of prescription" or "prescriptive periods." A common law legal system might have a statute limiting the time for prosecution of crimes called misdemeanors to two years after the offense occurred. In that statute, if a person is discovered to have committed a misdemeanor three years ago, the time has expired for the prosecution of the misdemeanor.
General Agreement on Tariffs and Trade	The General Agreement on Tariffs and Trade was the outcome of the failure of negotiating governments to create the International Trade Organization (ITO.) GATT was formed in 1947 and lasted until 1994, when it was replaced by the World Trade Organization. The Bretton Woods Conference had introduced the idea for an organization to regulate trade as part of a larger plan for economic recovery after World War II.
Tariff	A Tariff is a duty imposed on goods when they are moved across a political boundary. They are usually associated with protectionism, the economic policy of restraining trade between nations. For political reasons, Tariff s are usually imposed on imported goods, although they may also be imposed on exported goods.
Patent application	A patent application is a request pending at a patent office for the grant of a patent for the invention described and claimed by that application. An application consists of a description of the invention (the patent specification), together with official forms and correspondence relating to the application. The term patent application is also used to refer to the process of applying for a patent, or to the patent specification itself.
Patent Cooperation Treaty	The Patent Cooperation Treaty is an international patent law treaty, concluded in 1970. It provides a unified procedure for filing patent applications to protect inventions in each of its Contracting States A patent application filed under the Patent Cooperation Treaty is called an international application or Patent Cooperation Treaty application.

Chapter 4. Part IV The Law of Patents

Chapter 4. Part IV The Law of Patents

Disclosure	Disclosure means the giving out of information, either voluntarily or to be in compliance with legal regulations or workplace rules.

- In Computer security, full disclosure means disclosing full information about vulnerabilities.
- In computing, disclosure widget
- Journalism, full disclosure refers to disclosing the interests of the writer which may bear on the subject being written about, for example, if the writer has worked with an interview subject in the past.
- Psychology, disclosure refers talking to others about one"s feelings.

- In law:
    - The law of England and Wales, disclosure refers to a process that may form part of legal proceedings, whereby parties inform to other parties the existence of any relevant documents that are, or have been, in their control. This compares with the process known as discovery in the course of legal proceedings in the United States.
    - In U.S. civil procedure (litigation rules for civil cases), disclosure is a stage prior to trial. In civil cases, each party must disclose to the opposing party the following: names of witnesses which it may use to support its side, copies of documents (or mere description of these documents) in its control which it may use to support its side, computation of damages claimed, and certain insurance information. disclosure is related to, but technically prior to, the discovery stage.
    - In Company law (known as "corporate law" in the United States), disclosure refers to giving out information about public or limited companies or their officers, which might be kept secret if the company was a private company or a partnership.

- In real property transactions, disclosure refers to providing to a buyer information known to the seller or broker/agent concerning the condition or other aspects of real property that would affect the property"s value or desirability. These rules regarding what information must be disclosed, and whether the information must be disclosed even if a buyer does not ask, vary from one jurisdiction to the next. |
| Petition | A petition is a request to change something, most commonly made to a government official or public entity. petition s to a deity are a form of prayer.
In the colloquial sense, a petition is a document addressed to some official and signed by numerous individuals. |

Chapter 4. Part IV The Law of Patents

Chapter 4. Part IV The Law of Patents

Distinctiveness	Trademark distinctiveness is an important concept in the law governing trademarks and service marks. A trademark may be eligible for registration, or registrable, if amongst other things it performs the essential trademark function, and has distinctive character. Registrability can be understood as a continuum, with "inherently distinctive" marks at one end, "generic" and "descriptive" marks with no distinctive character at the other end, and "suggestive" and "arbitrary" marks lying between these two points.
Copyright	Copyright gives the creator of an original work exclusive right for a certain time period in relation to that work, including its publication, distribution and adaptation; after which time the work is said to enter the public domain. Copyright applies to any expressible form of an idea or information that is substantive and discrete and fixed in a medium. Some jurisdictions also recognize "moral rights" of the creator of a work, such as the right to be credited for the work.
Affidavit	An Affidavit is a formal sworn statement of fact, signed by the author, who is called the affiant or deponent, and witnessed as to the authenticity of the affiant"s signature by a taker of oaths, such as a notary public or commissioner of oaths. The name is Medieval Latin for he has declared upon oath. An Affidavit is a type of verified statement or showing, or in other words, it contains a verification, meaning it is under oath or penalty of perjury, and this serves as evidence to its veracity and is required for court proceedings.
Dispute	Controversy is a state of prolonged public dispute or debate usually concerning a matter of opinion. The term originates circa 1384 from Latin controversia, as a composite of controversus - "turned in an opposite direction," from contra - "against" - and vertere - to turn, or versus , hence, "to turn against." Benford"s law of controversy, as expressed by science-fiction author Gregory Benford in 1980, states: "Passion is inversely proportional to the amount of real (true) information available." In other words, the more untruths the more controversy there is, and the more truths the less controversy there is. A controversy is always the result of either ignorance (lack of sufficient true information), misinformation, misunderstandings, half-truths, distortions, bias or prejudice, deliberate lies or fabrications (disinformation), opposed underlying motives or purposes (sometimes masked or hidden), or a combination of these factors.
Independent contractor	An Independent contractor is a natural person, business, or corporation which provides goods or services to another entity under terms specified in a contract or within a verbal agreement. Unlike an employee, an Independent contractor does not work regularly for an employer but works as and when required, during which time she or he may be subject to the Law of Agency. Independent contractor s are usually paid on a freelance basis.
Personal property	Personal property is a type of property. In the common law systems Personal property may also be called chattels or personalty. It is distinguished from real property, or real estate.

Chapter 4. Part IV The Law of Patents

Chapter 4. Part IV The Law of Patents

Personal property may be classified in a variety of ways. Tangible Personal property refers to any type of property that can generally be moved (i.e., it is not attached to real property or land), touched or felt. These generally include items such as furniture, clothing, jewelry, art, writings, or household goods. In some cases, there can be formal title documents that show the ownership and transfer rights of that property after a person"s death (for example, motor vehicles, boats, etc.) In many cases, however, tangible Personal property will not be "titled" in an owner"s name and is presumed to be whatever property he or she was in possession of at the time of his or her death. Intangible Personal property or "intangibles" refers to Personal property that cannot actually be moved, touched or felt, but instead represents something of value such as negotiable instruments, securities, goods, and intangible assets including chose in action.

Shop right

Shop right, in United States patent law, is an implied license under which a firm may use a patented invention, invented by an employee who was working within the scope of their employment, using the firms" equipment, or inventing at the firms" expense. Even if the employee never assigned rights to the firm, a court of law may find that the firm has the right to make use of the invention, and thus can not be sued by the employee for patent infringement. This will allow the firm to attempt to capitalize on the value of the patent, as the firm is allowed to use the object of the patent in the routine operation of its business without royalty payments.

Federal Rules of Civil Procedure

The Federal Rules of Civil Procedure are rules governing civil procedure in United States district (federal) courts, that is, court procedures for civil suits. The FRCP are promulgated by the United States Supreme Court pursuant to the Rules Enabling Act, and then approved by the United States Congress. The Court"s modifications to the rules are usually based on recommendations from the Judicial Conference of the United States, the federal judiciary"s internal policy-making body.

Infringement

Infringement, when used alone, has several possible meanings in the English language. In a legal context, an infringement refers to the violation of a law or a right. This includes intellectual property infringements such as:

- copyright infringement
- patent infringement
- trademark infringement
- civel building infringement

Doctrine of exhaustion

Under the Doctrine of exhaustion the first unrestricted sale of a patented item exhausts the patentee"s control over that particular item. It generally is asserted as an affirmative defense to charges of patent infringement, but less commonly is asserted affirmatively in a declaratory judgment action.

Chapter 4. Part IV The Law of Patents

Chapter 4. Part IV The Law of Patents

	In other words, it is a concept in intellectual property law whereby an intellectual property owner will lose or "exhaust" certain rights after the first use of the subject matter which is the subject of intellectual property rights.
International Trade	International trade is exchange of capital, goods, and services across international borders or territories. In most countries, it represents a significant share of gross domestic product (GDP.) While International trade has been present throughout much of history, its economic, social, and political importance has been on the rise in recent centuries.
International Trade Commission	The United States International Trade Commission is an independent, non-partisan, quasi-judicial, federal agency of the United States that provides trade expertise to both the legislative and executive branches. Further, the agency determines the impact of imports on U.S. industries and directs actions against certain unfair trade practices, such as dumping, patent, trademark, and copyright infringement. The US International Trade Commission was established by the U.S. Congress in 1916 as the U.S. Tariff Commission (the Trade Act of 1974 changed its name to the U.S. International Trade Commission, the agency has broad investigative powers on matters of trade.
Patent infringement	Patent infringement is the performance of a prohibited act with respect to a patented invention without permission from the patent holder. Permission may typically be granted in the form of a licence. The acts may vary by jurisdiction, but typically include using or selling the patented invention.
Doctrine of equivalents	The Doctrine of equivalents is a legal rule in most of the world"s patent systems that allows a court to hold a party liable for patent infringement even though the infringing device or process does not fall within the literal scope of a patent claim, but nevertheless is equivalent to the claimed invention. U.S. judge Learned Hand has described its purpose as being "to temper unsparing logic and prevent an infringer from stealing the benefit of the invention". Royal Typewriter Co.
Estoppel	Estoppel is a legal doctrine at common law, where a party is barred from claiming or denying an argument on an equitable ground. Estoppel complements the requirement of consideration in contract law. In general, Estoppel protects an aggrieved party, if the counter-party induced an expectation from the aggrieved party, and the aggrieved party reasonably relied on the expectation and would suffer detriment if the expectation is not met.
Defenses	In the field of criminal law there are a variety of conditions that will tend to negate elements of a crime (particularly the intent element), known as defenses. The label may be apt in jurisdictions where the accused may be assigned some burden before a tribunal. However, in many jurisdictions, the entire burden to prove a crime is on the government, which also must prove the absence of these defenses, where implicated.
Compensatory damages	Compensatory damages are paid to compensate the claimant for loss, injury, or harm suffered by another"s breach of duty.

Chapter 4. Part IV The Law of Patents

Chapter 4. Part IV The Law of Patents

	On a breach of contract by a defendant, a court generally awards the sum which would restore the injured party to the economic position that he or she expected from performance of the promise or promises .
	When it is either not possible or desirable to award damages measured in that way, a court may award money damages designed to restore the injured party to the economic position that he or she had occupied at the time the contract was entered, or designed to prevent the breaching party from being unjustly enriched
Punitive damages	Punitive Damages are damages not awarded in order to compensate the plaintiff, but in order to reform or deter the defendant and similar persons from pursuing a course of action such as that which damaged the plaintiff.
	punitive Damages are often awarded where compensatory damages are deemed an inadequate remedy. The court may impose them to prevent under-compensation of plaintiffs, to allow redress for undetectable torts and taking some strain away from the criminal justice system.
Litigation	The conduct of a lawsuit is called Litigation.
	Rules of criminal or civil procedure govern the conduct of a lawsuit in the common law adversarial system of dispute resolution. Procedural rules are additionally constrained/informed by separate statutory laws, case law, and constitutional provisions that define the rights of the parties to a lawsuit , though the rules will generally reflect this legal context on their face.
American Arbitration Association	The American Arbitration Association is a private enterprise in the business of arbitration, and one of several arbitration organizations that administers arbitration proceedings. The American Arbitration Association also administers mediation and other forms of alternative dispute resolution. The International Centre for Dispute Resolution (ICDR), established in 1996, administers international arbitration proceedings initiated under the institution"s rules.
Arbitration	Arbitration, a form of alternative dispute resolution (ADR), is a legal technique for the resolution of disputes outside the courts, wherein the parties to a dispute refer it to one or more persons (the "arbitrators", "arbiters" or "arbitral tribunal"), by whose decision (the "award") they agree to be bound. It is a settlement technique in which a third party reviews the case and imposes a decision that is legally binding for both sides. Other forms of ADR include mediation (a form of settlement negotiation facilitated by a neutral third party) and non-binding resolution by experts.
Dispute Resolution	Dispute resolution is the process of resolving disputes between parties.

Chapter 4. Part IV The Law of Patents

Chapter 4. Part IV The Law of Patents

Methods of Dispute resolution include:

- lawsuits (litigation)
- arbitration
- collaborative law
- mediation
- conciliation
- many types of negotiation
- facilitation

One could theoretically include violence or even war as part of this spectrum, but Dispute resolution practitioners do not usually do so; violence rarely ends disputes effectively, and indeed, often only escalates them. Some individuals, notably Joseph Stalin, have stated that all problems emanate from man, and absent man, no problems ensue. Hence, violence could theoretically end disputes, but alongside it, life.

Agreement on Trade Related Aspects of Intellectual Property Rights	The Agreement on Trade Related Aspects of Intellectual Property Rights is an international agreement administered by the World Trade Organization (WTO) that sets down minimum standards for many forms of intellectual property (IP) regulation. It was negotiated at the end of the Uruguay Round of the General Agreement on Tariffs and Trade (GATT) in 1994. Specifically, TRIPS contains requirements that nations" laws must meet for: copyright rights, including the rights of performers, producers of sound recordings and broadcasting organizations; geographical indications, including appellations of origin; industrial designs; integrated circuit layout-designs; patents; monopolies for the developers of new plant varieties; trademarks; trade dress; and undisclosed or confidential information.
Intellectual Property	Intellectual property are legal property rights over creations of the mind, both artistic and commercial, and the corresponding fields of law. Under intellectual property law, owners are granted certain exclusive rights to a variety of intangible assets, such as musical, literary, and artistic works; ideas, discoveries and inventions; and words, phrases, symbols, and designs. Common types of intellectual property include copyrights, trademarks, patents, industrial design rights and trade secrets.
Trust	In common law legal systems, a trust is an arrangement whereby property (including real, tangible and intangible) is managed by one person (or persons, or organizations) for the benefit of another. A trust is created by a settlor, who entrusts some or all of his or her property to people of his choice (the trustees.) The trustees hold legal title to the trust property (or trust corpus), but they are obliged to hold the property for the benefit of one or more individuals or organizations (the beneficiary, a.k.a. cestui que use or cestui que trust), usually specified by the settlor, who hold equitable title.

Chapter 4. Part IV The Law of Patents

Chapter 4. Part IV The Law of Patents

Business method patents	Business method patents are a class of patents which disclose and claim new methods of doing business. This includes new types of e-commerce, insurance, banking, tax compliance etc. Business method patents are a relatively new species of patent and there have been several reviews investigating the appropriateness of patenting business methods.
European Patent Convention	The Convention on the Grant of European Patents of 5 October 1973, commonly known as the European Patent Convention , is a multilateral treaty instituting the European Patent Organisation and providing an autonomous legal system according to which European patents are granted. The term European patent is used to refer to patents granted under the European Patent Convention. However, after grant a European patent is not a unitary right, but a group of essentially independent nationally-enforceable, nationally-revocable patents, subject to central revocation or narrowing as a group pursuant to two types of unified, post-grant procedures: a time-limited opposition procedure, which can be initiated by any person except the patent proprietor, and limitation and revocation procedures, which can be initiated by the patent proprietor only.

Chapter 4. Part IV The Law of Patents

CPSIA information can be obtained at www.ICGtesting.com
Printed in the USA
269125BV00002B/107/P

9 781616 987633